Contents

AF119454

Welcome to the cards	1
Why use these cards?	2
What is intersectionality?	4
What are intersectional factors?	6
What is intersectional design?	8
What is design?	10
How to use the cards	14
Design activities	22
Case study index	28
References	30

Welcome to the Intersectional Design Cards

These cards are designed to help teams explore and develop intersectional design solutions.

How might you use them?
- To start a **conversation**
- To **critique** your product, experience, or service
- To **brainstorm** ideas

The deck includes:
- Guide Booklet
- Set of Intersectional Factor Definition Cards
- Set of Design Question Cards
- Set of Case Study Cards

> The cards are also available online.
> Visit **www.intersectionaldesign.com**

Why use these cards?

- ✓ Navigate assumptions and biases to avoid designing to stereotypes.

- ✓ Integrate intersectional design thinking into your design work - from the beginning.

- ✓ Course correct.

- ✓ Identify new markets and business opportunities.

- ✓ Work towards building an equitable, sustainable, and just society.

The goal of these cards is to help you create an intersectional design cycle:

Designers
who question
social norms

Cultures
that challenge
social norms

Products
that embody social norms
and promote equity

Users
who rethink
social norms

What is intersectionality?

In 1989, legal scholar Kimberlé Crenshaw coined the term intersectionality to describe how multiple forms of discrimination intersect in Black women's lives in ways that are erased when sexism and racism are treated separately.

The principle emerged from the 1976 U.S. case DeGraffenreid v. General Motors (GM). The five Black women bringing the case argued they suffered compound discrimination. Prior to 1964, when the Civil Rights Act went into effect, GM regularly hired women for office and secretarial jobs. But, in practice, they hired only white women. At the same time, GM hired Black people on the manufacturing floor (assembling cars and the like), but, in practice, these were all men.

The Black women were hired into secretarial jobs only after 1964—and as the "last hired" were the "first fired". These women asked the court to consider that as Black women, the law did not protect them either as Black people or as women. The court refused to create a new class of "protected minorities" and these women, unfortunately, lost their case, but the principle of "intersectionality" was born.

Guide

What are intersectional factors?

Age
Disability
Educational Background
Ethnicity
Family Configuration
Gender
Geographic Location
Race
Sex
Sexuality
Social and Economic Status
Sustainability

Since 1989, intersectionality has broadened from gender and race, to describe multiple intersecting factors emerging from structural advantages and disadvantages in society. Intersecting factors may include age, social and economic status (SES), educational background, geographical location, etc. that interact to shape a person's or a group's experience and social opportunities.

Our design case studies include—but are not limited to—the twelve intersecting factors, listed at left.

Other factors may include appearance, language, political ideology, religion, immigration status, work background, Indigeneity, physical and mental health, and more.

> What other intersectinoal factors might be relevant?
> Email us at **feedback@intersectionaldesign.com**

What is intersectional design?

Intersectional Design drives innovation while supporting social justice and environmental sustainability. It's about getting the design right for people across all of society—from the very beginning.

An iconic example of intersectional design comes from facial recognition. Computer scientists Joy Boulamwini and Timnit Gebru's "Gender Shades" study analyzed gender and race to discover that the system could not see Black women's faces. The system worked so poorly that one team member—a Black woman—had to put on a White mask for it to see her.

This would not have been known without intersectional analysis. Gender analysis revealed that the systems performed better on men's faces than on women's faces. Race analysis showed that the systems performed better on lighter skin than darker skin. Intersectional analysis demonstrated that the system performed worst for Black women. Error rates were 35% for darker-skinned women, 12% for darker-skinned men, 7% for lighter-skinned women, and less than 1% for lighter-skinned men.

The fix? The team developed a new database to create a system that worked well for everyone.

What is design?

Our definition of design is organized into four interrelated levels. These levels scale up from physical objects to cultural trends.

This expanded definition of design encourages designers to consider where their products make an impact and how they can improve the inclusivity of their work.

In this deck, we reference **four levels of design**:

 01 Form & Function

The look and feel of a design, its physical qualities and characteristics, and the impact of its materials and production on the environment.

 02 Experiences & Services

User/customer experience, brand interaction, business models, strategies, and design decision-making.

 03 Systems & Infrastructures

Systems thinking, sustainability, interdisciplinarity, networks, and databases.

 04 Paradigms & Purpose

Conceptual frameworks, models, worldviews, major cultural themes, archetypes, ideologies, and mindsets.

Examples of design levels

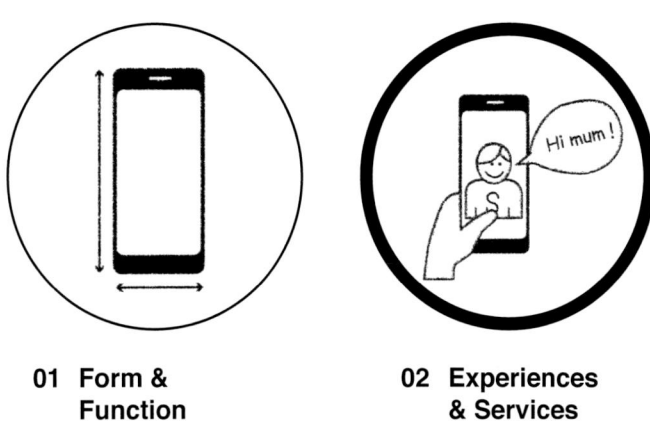

01 Form & Function

02 Experiences & Services

Today, we recognize that design encompasses many different things. Take the example of the smart phone. Design might mean the look and feel of the device in your hand, the experience of video chatting or using a virtual assistant...

03 Systems & Infrastructures

04 Paradigms & Purpose

...the network of hardware and software that the device connects to, and/or the cultural trends that emerge through using the device in new and unforeseen ways.

These cards are designed to help teams explore, analyze, and develop intersectional design solutions.

Step 1

Start here.

Read through this together as a group:

Intersectional design is a new and evolving methodology. Engaging in conversations with colleagues about different social factors—race, ethnicity, sexuality—can be sensitive. Establish ground rules to feel safe and to have a respectful dialogue.

Some of the terms might be new to people on your team. Or people might have different definitions or understandings. For example, the words "race" and "ethnicity" have different, sometimes overlapping meanings and are used, or explicitly not used, in different countries. Some language used in the cards might be uncomfortable or mean different things to different generations or cultures.

Exploring the definitions can help your team establish a shared language before applying them to your intersectional design practice.

Step 2

Establish ground rules.

We suggest these rules:

- Lead with openness, care, and respect.

- Focus on listening. Have one conversation at a time, don't speak over others, and try to balance the contributions from individuals.

- Build on each other's ideas, noting as you go the different intersecting factors that surface in the conversation. Allow the conversation to expand and explore multiple intersecting factors.

- Avoid rushing to get to solutions. Take your time understanding how intersectionality works.

- Mistakes are likely to be made. Be sensitive to each other's learning experience.

- Respect all confidentiality or anonymity requests made by the group and/or individuals.

Are there other rules that should be included?

Email us at **feedback@intersectionaldesign.com**

Step 3

Set up the cards.

Organize the cards into their three sets:

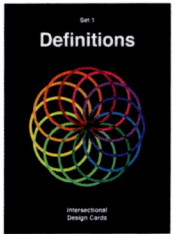

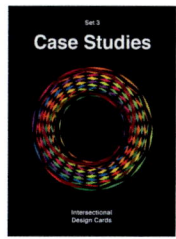

Set 1: Definitions

This set includes a definition of intersectionality and 12 intersectional factor definitions.

Set 2: Questions

This set includes the design levels map and 12 design questions.

Set 3: Case Studies

This set includes 16 case studies and an index.

Step 4

Identify your goal.

The cards have been designed with a purposefully open structure. You can read through the whole deck, take a single case to review as a team, or spend time exploring a key question in depth.

What would you like to accomplish?
To get you started we suggest three ways to use the cards:

Start a conversation.
Create a space conducive for open conversation. We start with definitions because people come in with their own biases, and it's good to level-set.

Critique your work.
Use the cards to take a critical look at your product, experience, and/or service.

Brainstorm ideas.
Think broadly about how users with different intersectional characteristics will be served by your product, experience, or service. Who have you overlooked? How might your design improve by including them?

Step 5

Try it out.

Decide which path you want to explore, and follow the directions for that activity.

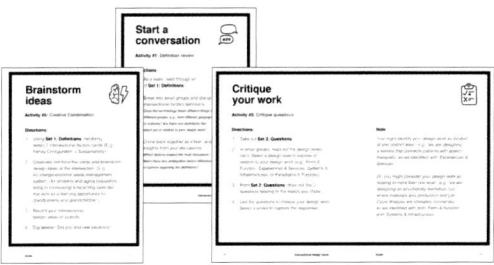

For each of these activities you should allow approximately 45 minutes. Or, you could connect the activities together for a full 2+ hour session. Depending on what you wish to accomplish, you might want to design your own workshop.

> Let us know how the activities went.
> Email us at **feedback@intersectionaldesign.com**

Step 6

Reflect.

It's crucial to build time for reflection into or immediately following these activities. Louie Montoya, d.school designer and educator, cautions, "most 'design malpractice' happens when people are acting but not reflecting."

We suggest the following feedback framework:

Before the workshop, I expected..

During the workshop, I learned....

After the workshop, I plan to apply what I learned by...

Additional reflection questions:

- How did that go?

- What are three key takeaways from this session?

- What do you feel the team needs to focus on next as a result of this workshop?

- What do you feel your team needs to learn more about?

- Where does your product or service succeed across intersectional factors?

- How might your design change as social and environmental relations change in the coming years?

Start a conversation

Activity #1: Review the definitions

Directions:

1. As a team, read through all of **Set 1: Definitions**.

2. Break into small groups and discuss the intersectional factors definitions.
   Does the terminology mean different things to different people, e.g., from different geographies or cultures? Are there any definitions that stand out in relation to your design work?

3. Come back together as a team and share insights from your discussions.
   Which factors created the most discussion? Were there any ambiguities and/or differences of opinion regarding the definitions?

Start a conversation

Activity #2: Apply the definitions

Directions:

1. In small groups, using **Set 1: Definitions**, select factors that highlight the intersections where your product, experience, or service is doing well, or where it is falling short.

2. Have you identified any intersecting factors that are not in the cards? Fill in a blank card.

3. Each group share the intersections that they have identified.

4. Discuss them as a whole team. Agree as a team on 3 or more key intersecting factors to take forward to the critique your work stage.

Critique your work

Activity #3: Ask critical questions

Directions:

1. Take out **Set 2: Questions**.

2. In small groups, read out the design levels card. Select a design level to explore in relation to your design work (e.g., Form & Function, Experiences & Services, Systems & Infrastructures, or Paradigms & Purpose).

3. From **Set 2: Questions**, draw out the 3 questions relating to the level/s you chose.

4. Use the questions to critique your design work. Select a scribe to capture the responses.

Note

You might identify your design work as located at one distinct level. For example: "We are designing a service that connects patients with speech therapists, so we identified with 'Experiences & Services.'"

Or, you might consider your design work as relating to more than one level. For example: "We are designing an eco-friendly menstrual cup, where materials and production and Life Cycle Analysis are intimately connected, so we identified with both 'Form & Function' and 'Systems & Infrastructure.'"

Critique your work

Activity #4: Review the case studies

Directions:

1. Pull out a case study related to your selected level/s from **Set 3: Case Studies**.

2. Pull out the case study's intersectional factors from **Set 1: Definitions**. Discuss.

3. Come back to your own work, identify existing or potential intersectional factors (or use your previously selected 3 intersectional factors if you have already undertaken the "Review the definitions" activity).

4. As a whole team, use our case study card as a template, write out and illustrate your own "case study card" that summarizes your design, highlighting your design level/s and your intersecting factors. Bring this card along to all subsequent design meetings.

Brainstorm ideas

Activity #5: Get creative

Directions:

1. Using **Set 1: Definitions**, randomly select 2 intersectional factors cards (E.g. Family Configuration + Sustainability)

2. Creatively combine the cards and brainstorm design ideas at the intersection. (E.g. An intergenerational waste management system - for students and aging population living in co-housing/ a recycling calendar that acts as a learning opportunity for grandparents and grandchildren.)

3. Record your intersectional design ideas on post-its.

4. Dig deeper. Did you find new solutions?

Case study index

01 Form & Function

1.1 Inclusive Crash Test Dummies: Age, Ethnicity, Gender, Sex

1.2 Facial Recognition: Gender, Sex

1.3 Pulse Oximeter: Race, Sex

1.4 Data Biases in Machine Learning: Ethnicity, Geographic Location

02 Experiences & Services

2.1 Osteoporosis in Men: Ethnicity, Gender, Geographic Location, Sex

2.2 Virtual Assistants: Gender, Ethnicity, Sexuality

2.3 Smart Mobility: Age, Gender, Sexuality

2.4 Implicit Bias in Media: Gender, Race, Sexuality, Social and Economic Status (SES)

To read the complete case studies, please visit:

www.genderedinnovations.stanford.com

03 Systems & Infrastructures

3.1 Menstrual Cups: Gender, Sex, Sustainability

3.2 Water Infrastructure: Educational Background, Gender

3.3 Transportation Planning: Family Configuration, Gender

3.4 Playgrounds: Age, Gender, Sexuality

04 Paradigms & Purpose

4.1 Social Robots: Disability, Gender, Race

4.2 Marine Science: Sex, Social and Economic Status (SES), Sustainability

4.3 Sports Hijabs: Ethnicity, Gender

4.4 Haptic Technology: Age, Ethnicity, Gender

We'd love to hear your intersectional design examples.
Email us at **feedback@intersectionaldesign.com**

References

Bailey, I. J. (2018). How Implicit Bias Works in Journalism - https://niemanreports.org/articles/how-implicit-bias-works-in-journalism/

Buolamwini, J. & Gebru, T. (2018). Gender shades: Intersectional accuracy disparities in commercial gender classification. In Conference on fairness, accountability and transparency, 77-91. And the video: Gender Shades. http://gendershades.org/

Crenshaw, K. (1989). Demarginalizing the intersection of race and sex: A black feminist critique of antidiscrimination doctrine, feminist theory and antiracist politics. In University of Chicago Legal Forum, 140(1), 139-167.

Feiner, J. R. et al. (2007). Dark skin decreases the accuracy of pulse oximeters at low oxygen saturation: The effects of oximeter probe type and gender. Anesthesia & Analgesia, 105(6), S18-S23.

Garg, N., Schiebinger, L., Jurafsky, D. & Zou, J. (2018). Word embeddings quantify 100 years of gender and ethnic stereotypes. Proceedings of the National Academy of Sciences, 115(16), E3635-E3644.

University of Michigan Transportation Research Institute - http://humanshape.org/AdultShape/

Keyes, O. (2018). The misgendering machines: Trans/HCI implications of automatic gender recognition. Proceedings of the ACM on Human-Computer Interaction, 2 (CSCW).